A LIFE OF LOVE

How to Create Relationships You Want

James Allen Hanrahan

With

Dr. Pat Allen

DEDICATION

To my beloved wife, Una

CONTENTS

PART I – INTENTION

PART II – ENERGY

PART III – STORIES

PART IV – COMMUNICATION

PART 1 - INTENTION

TIMING

They say timing is everything. When the student is ready the teacher appears. The work is in the preparation, then love suddenly appears. The tree seems to fall with one blow and the axe man knows it was all the strikes before.

PREPARATION

It's been said that love appears when you least expect it, like an overnight sensation. Yet, the overnight sensation knows the preparation.

Timing plays an important role in love.

"When individuals are looking for adventure craving to leave home, lonely, displaced in a foreign country, passing into a new stage in life or financially and psychologically ready to share themselves or start a family they become susceptible." – Helen Fisher, *Anatomy of Love.*

Love begins when the story ends, when the old story ends. When the life script that has unconsciously run our lives suddenly becomes too painfully obvious to continue, we're ready. When we're sick and tired of being sick and tired; when the pain of not changing is greater than the pain of change.

There are no accidents. Every blow, every misstep is right on time. Rumi was once asked to define

Sufism. He said it is "Joy at sudden disappointment."

The life script is a big loss. It's the safety net that makes us fall, fall into old habits, old ways of being, sabotaging ourselves when the time is right.

Your life script is your mantra, usually written at an early age by a trauma. It's often one line. It can be found out many times with one question. For a man the question is what was your mother like? For a woman the question is what was your father like? The length of time to answer reflects the depth of the wound. The answer is always simple and it's always profound.

My answer was I could only take care of myself—not a recipe for love. I formulated this answer, this mantra at the age of 12. My mother had been in a car accident and was in the hospital. My father OD'd on prescription drugs and alcohol and he was in the hospital. As I stood there by myself, I decided I couldn't take care of anyone else, I could only take care of myself.

Timing is everything. One blow to the psyche writes the script we live. Preparation heals. Preparation until the love we pour in overcomes the love that has poured out.

Awakening comes with the realization, "Oh, my God, look what I've done to myself." I've kept myself in jail, kept myself small, afraid of my own shadow, afraid of everything and nothing at all.

Insanity is doing the same thing over and over again and expecting different results.

This time the blow works in our favor. The last straw breaks the camel's back. When the pain of staying stagnant outweighs the pain of becoming, we're ripe; the fruit falls from the tree when the time is right.

THE MISSION

We're on a mission to find love. If you don't think we're on a mission, explain the explosion of online dating. Two hundred million single people on a mission. We're definitely on a mission. It's in our DNA. We're designed to procreate, designed to obey our inner promptings.

At this point one can question the design. We're getting in our own way. I've tried to understand why this mission is so hard. We have collectively decided it's a numbers' game. We've decided to use numbers to overcome the odds.

Turns out I'm suddenly a member of www.match.com. I didn't even sign up; I'm married. However, www.match.com decided to sign me up, although they assure me I signed up and they're sending me my latest matches.

Obviously they know my preferences because they're sending me everyone and everything with a first name in my area. After all, it's a numbers' game. Maybe they're right. After all, how many sperm did it take to fertilize one egg? They do have statistical backing on this one.

Also, www.chemistry.com just sent me an e-mail. They're all on to me. They have a questionnaire to determine my love type. Now that's legit. These people seem much happier with a legit title instead

4

of just a first name. I think we're getting somewhere.

The age old philosophical question: "Who am I?" has been answered. Technology has given me what pheromones, hormones and eye contact could never have given me—a title.

I now have a proven strategy to use in the numbers' game. With this much technology I don't know how online dating can not keep growing exponentially. Over population looms as a concern. Where is all this going?

To think in the Dark Ages all I said was hello. Now I have a personality or at least a way to test it.

HEARD AND KNOWN

We have two basic needs, to be heard and known.
We gather our tones, gestures and facial expressions
from others. We thrive in relationship. We need to
be touched. Touch bonds us with oxytocin.
Serotonin rises to calm us. We crave the dopamine
rush of infatuation or the deep longing of
norepinephrine. If we can outlast these gatekeepers
we can come home to being heard and known. Our
serotonin kicks in when we're at home when our
being recognizes we are loved. The highs keep us
chasing for elusive perfection.

Initial attraction is a natural amphetamine. It brings
us to life with the richness of the moment. The
windows fly open. We fall in love through the
senses—touch, taste, smell, vision, hearing.

Men fall in love with their eyes; women with their
ears. Seen and heard.

We purposely cross paths to collide, to combust,
knowing we can't do it alone. We need spark, we
need ignition to breathe. We come alive when
someone takes our breath away, when our thinking
becomes clouded by the rush of our senses.

Touch is a necessity; babies can't survive without it.
We're programmed in the first three months of life
by touch. We go feral without it. The need

continues throughout life. Touch grounds us. It keeps us from flying off into our heads.

We instinctively and intuitively know love. Kids and dogs gravitate towards it. The pool of our being waits for it, the recognition.

When people begin to attract to each other they begin to sync up. They first start to square their shoulders off to each other preparing to dance. The mating dance is truly a dance. We mirror each other. She takes a drink, he takes a drink. And on and on it goes. Each movement synchronizes us into a rhythm.

We all unconsciously seek rhythm. We unconsciously understand how important it is. It's in our DNA. When groups of women become friends their monthly cycles begin to sync up. Studies have shown that just the scent of a man placed under the nose regularly, three to five times a week, will regulate a woman's cycle.

We dance for a reason. We look for a reason. An old saying is "The eyes are the windows of the soul". The soul knows what it's looking for when it sees it. We're programmed for recognition. Our mirror neurons search for congruity.

When people say they don't need love they're mistaken. Their heads have talked them out of it for the moment. Yet, their bodies know better. A mere glimpse drives them back into the eternal. Love is all there is.

Energy is all there is. Our bodies know it. Our heart knows it. Our souls recognize we're not alone. Our eyes are our portal. Our ears are our wings. We're transported by our love songs. We repeat what he or she said, looking for the subtle clues which can be read.

We drive to the finish line in our head: love.

We live in anticipation knowing it's just a matter of time. Our involution has planted a seed in us. We grow to its fruition. We dance to its beat. It sends us in our direction, each totally unique. We're driven back to the beginning or wherever we got lost. We're healed by the meaning. We become willing to pay the cost.

Escape from freedom comes to mind. We love because it's an imperative to be heard, to be known.

LONGING

I have a dream, a great longing that has become my drummer. It beats in the winter and beats in the summer. The crest of my emotions longing to be home.

Some of us are norepinepherine addicts. We long for love. Or shall I say we long for longing. The carrot on a stick. We follow the illusion to keep it out of reach. How many people have gotten what they wanted to their utter disappointment? The rationale is I was mistaken, this is not it.

We can't stand the satisfaction. It kills the high. When we run on norepinepherine it's a long ride. Getting off kills the buzz. We long because longing is where the adrenalin is.

I've heard that the worst thing that can happen is to have your dreams come true. Sounds absurd until you've tried it. Ask lottery winners. It typically destroys their lives. Ground is so important. We'll do anything to get back to it.

We're fundamentally built from the ground up. We learn our taste for longing by discounting elusive people growing up. We follow our leaders. We beat to their rhythm searching for clues on how love is given.

Chase me, don't catch me. Keep me on the hook. How many of you have left someone because they loved you? The unrequited is how we treat ourselves. We learn to discount the genuine. We fight to stay afloat even when we're buoyant.

The craving brain wires for more highs. We develop a taste for dissatisfaction. It becomes a way of life.

Longing seems rational to no one but you. Your friends look on in amazement. That's when you're not secretive. It's usually a best kept secret, best shared alone. Longing hates to be interrupted.

Addiction is defined as an allergy of the body, a compulsion of the mind. We always have chemistry. The question is: "What kind?" How well do we handle being well? For some of us it's an acquired taste. Well being is not a first choice, it's not high enough, not low enough.

Longing is a horseless rider going nowhere, spiraling in circles of stagnation. There's safety in the known. It tranquilizes us. We argue for our limitations. They're our oldest friends. We don't want the happy ending. We want something that doesn't end.

A companion of compulsion. Compulsion is our friend. When the light comes on and the show is over our face is flushed from getting nowhere. For all its dramatics we haven't changed at all.

I wish for you a happy ending, a fight to the finish. I know it's there. Right from the beginning. It's why you're in it.

CHEMISTRY 101

Our bodies are coded to find what we're looking for. We're looking for chemistry. We have chemistry inside us in our DNA. When we get within 30 inches of someone our bodies begin to go to work. Through the sense of smell we pick up pheromones from the other person containing their DNA.

What are we looking for? If you're a woman you're looking for someone a little like your dad and a little not like your dad. Too much like your dad is taboo. Too much not like your dad is alien.

Have you ever had the experience where a person is perfect on paper? They have nine of the 10 things you're looking for. They fit your profile to a T. They even sound good on the phone. With great anticipation you go to meet them and nothing. You feel nothing. No chemistry.

Chemistry makes your heart pound, your body sweat, your eyes dilate. Like how it did with your old boyfriend, the one with no job who cheated on you. Chemistry is body to body. It's lust to lust.

Chemistry knows something you don't know, DNA. Is chemistry foolproof? How many people have had chemistry with someone who's the worst thing for you? Maybe it's your pheromones' fault. Or maybe while those red flags were going off you decided…

well, decided would have meant you thought about it. To take it one step further you touched. You forgot what your mother said to you as a little kid: don't touch. Touch takes you to the next level; you bond. Chemically, hormonally it's called oxytocin. Oxytocin is far more indiscriminate. Touch rules bodies.

When you have sex with someone you will bond. The intensity will depend on your age. Young women and older men bond. They're driven by estrogen. Young men and older women don't bond. They're driven by testosterone and progesterone.

How many people have bonded to people they don't even like? You know how you did it? You touched. And more likely you had sex with them before you knew them. It's ironic but people often have sex to avoid intimacy.

Once your body bonds to a person through oxytocin good luck getting out of it. Because now all of your senses kick in—the smell of the them, the sound of their voice, the sight of them, the taste, the touch all trigger you. This is the reason people often have a hard time getting over someone because they don't. They rebound, they hear the voice then they see the person, etc. The only cure is time and abstinence, to refrain from seeing, touching, tasting, hearing or smelling. Painfully.

It will take at least eight weeks and up to two years. Painfully. Our bodies crave touch. It's a good thing. Oxytocin when administered properly with an appropriate person gives us a sense of well being. We're designed to bond.

The skillful questions are how, when and with whom. How we know is chemistry. It's body to body.

BAD CHEMISTRY

Bad chemistry sets you off, off the deep end. One of the best ways to get it is by choosing unreliable, uncommiting people or being one yourself. Many people feel a longing to be loved. While it's certainly dramatic, the high is a low. It's norepinephrine.

The downward spiral definitely gives you something to complain about. That's part of the attraction. The best part is the high. The low surging through your body, the chemistry. It stimulates adrenaline and is exciting. However, adrenaline is for short bursts. When it's sustained for long periods of time the body produces cortisol. Cortisol tears down your body, compromising your immune system.

People get love sick, and they can't eat, can't sleep, can't stop thinking about each other. If these symptoms are in the beginning they're euphoric. If they don't stop they'll create bad chemistry.

Bad chemistry can't get enough. It's never satiated because enough is not the goal. Lack is what drives it. Some people go insane to get what they want; then they don't want it when they get it because it defeats the purpose. Getting what you want ruins the high, the low. Who wants that?

This is the rat race that takes you down.

COMPATIBILITY

When you stop to think about it compatibility is mind to mind. It is to like. When your body is on fire this might not seem important. When your house burns down it is.

We're definitely playing with fire when we mate. The right person can take us to highs we only dream of. The wrong person—well we already know how that goes.

Like is underrated. Commonality does not invoke fireworks. That's the reason it's important, it's foundational. When we like someone they grow on us. They grow with us, our paths join, we have common interests. It can be as simple as geography. We both like to live in the same place, the same country.

Like is often underestimated. I joke with my friend. He says, "I just met a girl from Peru." I say, "Great. When are you moving to Peru?"

It can be as seemingly trivial as when you go to bed, when you get up, what kind of movies you like, common hobbies. Perhaps the biggest piece is how you spend your time—time alone, time together, time with other people.

Some people are extroverts; they like to be around people. They get their energy being around people.

Some people are introverts; they gather energy by being alone.

Like goes a long way. Like takes time, it takes objectivity, something chemistry often doesn't have.

Put together the pieces. I call it filling out the other 23 hours. Building a life together is not magical thinking; it's brick by brick, stone by stone, foundational. The basic foundation is agreement. People who can make and keep agreements are commitable.

When we like each other we begin to get on the same page, then we write the book. Commonality gives us a chance.

Long distance doesn't. Conflicting lifestyles doesn't. Conflicting values doesn't.

Common ground is simple. I like you. I like how you are. I like who you are. I like your house, your clothes, your car. I like you enough. Not perfect. Enough. You are someone I can laugh with.

We're looking for integrity, for soundness of mind and body. Someone we can resonate with, who hears us and sees us.

Physical beauty is packaging. We take the wrapper off to find the things we're looking for.

Like closes the distance step-by-step.

COMMUNICATION

The three Cs are chemistry, compatibility and communication. The three Cs are lust, like and love.

Chemistry no one can give you. You have it or you don't. Chemistry equals lust, body to body. It's instantaneous.

Compatibility takes more time. It's inquiry, it's finding out preferences, ways of being in the world, how you spend your time, where you spend your time, what's important to you. Compatibility equals like. It's mind to mind and takes time to discover.

The last C is communication. Communication equals love. When we love we make and keep agreements, we negotiate. We give up intimidating and seducing people with money and sex and make agreements.

If you don't want to give up anything, then stay single. Have sex once in a while. Keep your money and go home. Relationships are not for people who want everything. They're for people who want to share what they have. Share is where everything comes together. It's where our unique qualities mix.

Communication is being heard and known. It's intimacy. The only way you know you love yourself is by the commitments you're willing to make and keep. Communication is the ability to say what you mean and mean what you say. It's not mystery theatre. It's not the drama and game-playing of trying to figure out what he or she meant. It's not analysis. It's clear communication.

Communication is the ability to express your wants and don't wants in a respectful and cherishing way.

People who love talk; they talk for hours. A relationship is a conversation that doesn't end. The four signs of a loser in communication are: they're evasive, secretive, abrupt and condescending. Only fight with people you want to build with.

Avoid drama for drama's sake. Instead, find someone who's willing to fight with you for love's sake because those are the people who love you.

Communication equals love. Sharing, the ability to share our wants and don't wants with another human being with respect and cherishing. It means I care what you think and how you feel.

When a man is respected for his thinking he feels cherished. When a woman is cherished for her feelings she feels respected. We mirror each other.

Chemistry, compatibility, communication—we need all three. Chemistry and communication without compatibility equals lovers, sex partners. Chemistry and compatibility without communication equals fighters. Negative love. Compatibility and communication without chemistry equals friendship. For intimate, romantic relationships we need all three.

TO BE IN LOVE

To be in love, the question to ask is: Do we have enough chemistry, enough compatibility and enough communication skills? Enough is at least 51 percent; it's the tipping point. No one is perfect. Some days are better than others. All people are amazing. Given a chance they grow on us. The trick is to not discount them before they do.

Love makes people beautiful. Look at a pregnant mother. She glows. People in love laugh, they smile, they create endorphins. It's nature's beauty parlor. They say love is an elixir, a magic potion of invincibility. It sparks in infatuation. It kindles in compatibility. It flames in communication. This is where we get our warmth, our sustenance, our humanity.

Start small with eye contact and smiles. Talk. He who talks first is masculine. Set the tone you want. If you are the masculine, say what you think and what you want. That's it. Keep it simple. What you think and what you want. If you're the feminine say what you feel and what you don't want. That's it. It's that simple. It works. It's profound. Practice. Date people.

TYPES OF RELATIONSHIPS

There are three basic types of relationships. When you know the type of relationship you want you'll know what you're looking for. Convenient, codependent and covenant.

A convenient relationship is basically a 50/50 relationship where two independent people bring social and financial security and sensual and sexual security for a joint venture in the world. Both people typically work and share expenses. It's characterized by equality. The challenge with so much equality is to keep the relationship dynamic.

To keep the dynamic of masculine and feminine energy it's imperative to cross-talk; i.e., masculine energy says what it thinks and wants; feminine energy says what it feels and doesn't want. Remember this tool.

The second type is codependent, where one person is a 10 and the other person is a zero. One person gets cherished and respected, the other gets nothing. These relationships are usually created by people who exclude a part of themselves. Often one person plays the part of the adult/parent, the other plays the part of the child. These relationships are often quite dramatic. It's two dependent people symbiotically coming together to face a fearful world.

The third type is a covenant. It's two independent people who negotiate a mutual interdependency for a greater good to become a balanced unit in the world. In a covenant each person takes on a primary role for the greatest good of the team. One person is designated as the bread winner, one person the homemaker.

Men surrender their sexual independence, women their financial independence to create a dynamic interdependence.

Masculine energy by nature does good to feel good. Feminine energy feels good to do good. By "giving away" a piece of our independence we're able to create a whole greater than the sum of its parts. In other words, we love. This relationship allows for the greatest freedom of expression. It's lead and follow; cherish and respect; give and receive.

Once you decide the heading you want to be under, the style of relationship you want, you can begin to break down the components. There are four basic components: time, space, money and play.

Time. There are three basic types of time: me alone, us as a couple alone, us as a couple plus others.

First decide how much time you want to be alone or with others who aren't your significant other. For example, you can choose to be alone two days a week. Do the same with time as a couple alone. Then do the same for time as a couple social time.

Knowing these things about yourself before you start a relationship will give you a big head start. Remember, they're a starting point. They're flexible. When you get with another person you'll negotiate with them for a greater good.

Space. This is a big one. Figure out where you want to live, where you're willing to live. Are you willing to relocate? Are you willing to move in with someone or have them move in with you? These are nuts and bolts. Think ahead. Also private property. What's yours? What's mine? What's ours? Private space, closets, drawers, etc.

Maintenance responsibilities and chore responsibilities are part of space. Consider your strengths. Some people like to cook, some like to clean. Hopefully when you get together with someone some of these things will work out naturally, others will be negotiated.

Money. Mine, yours, ours. Think about how you want to work with money, how you want to share. Decide in advance. Know what you're comfortable with first.

Play. Again, me, we and us. What are your hobbies along with your partner, with others? All aspects fill in the pieces of the whole. The clearer you are about your wants and don't wants the easier it will be to negotiate with others.

Sexual play. Again, me, we and us. How often? With whom?

Get clear what your taste and rhythms are in all areas. Periodically revisit these areas because priorities change. Keep up with each other. Stay current and flexible.

COURTSHIP SYNERGY

Courtship energetically has direction; it's going somewhere. Often towards commitment, towards children, towards a long-term relationship. As such it circulates by way of giving and receiving. In a courtship yang energy gives concretely. Yin energy receives concretely and then gives back abstractly through appreciation.

Through this way of giving and receiving courtship energy replenishes itself and continues to flow synergistically in an unbroken circle.

In contrast, emotional dating is often a one-way street, often going the wrong way where the participants are ego dystonic or inside out. For example, a woman operating predominantly from her yang energy will give—give to please— typically sex or money or both; while a man operating predominantly from his yin energy will use and abuse. This causes the synergy to break down when she finds she really wants to be yin and/or he finds he really wants to be yang, as nature intended, before "life's script" training has undone nature's plan.

TYPES OF WOMEN AND MEN

With these directions in mind, let's look at three types of women and three types of men energetically and directionally.

First we have Wendy. Wendy is selfless. She gives her money and sex to men first with nothing in return. Energetically she's a one way street going the wrong way. Giver, Wendy, selfless.

Next we have the claw, the gold digger. The claw woman is selfish. She usually takes money without giving appreciation in return. Her mantra is give me more. She's also a one-way street going the wrong way. Taker, gold digger, selfish.

The last woman is a real woman called an anchor. She's self-centered, and as she loves herself she's able to receive concretely first, then give back abstractly, creating synergy through reciprocation. She's a two-way street.

Types of men. First we have the sugar daddy. Sugar daddy is selfless in that he doesn't love himself. He's a one-way giver, giving usually money with no appreciation in return. He's on a one-way street going the wrong way. Giver, sugar daddy, selfless.

Next we have Peter Pan. Peter Pan is selfish, he's a taker, usually of money and sex without giving anything concretely. He believes women, children and animals on the planet are here to serve his needs. He's also a one-way street going the wrong way. Taker, Peter Pan, selfish.

The last man is a real man. He's self-centered in that he loves himself. He's a receiver second, meaning he realizes women, animals, children and the planet are not here for his gratification. He has the ability to give concretely first, then receive abstractly by way of being appreciated for his giving. He's a two-way street.

PART II - ENERGY

YIN AND YANG ENERGY

How many people consider themselves to be androgynous? How many people know what it means to be androgynous?

The yin yang symbol is a Chinese symbol thousands of years old. It depicts energy—yang masculine, and yin feminine energy.

The large white portion represents yang energy. Yang energy has a male body; however, it has a yin soul. The soul of a man is called the anima. This is the work of Carl Jung. Yin energy, in contrast, depicted by the larger black area has a female body; however, it has a yang soul called the animus.

The answer to the question is that we're all androgynous. We're all a mixture of yin and yang energy somewhere along a continuum.

For men, at one end of the continuum, we have Mr. Macho. Mr. Macho exhibits masculine energy to the exclusion of his yin energy.

At the other extreme, we have Peter Pan. Peter Pan exhibits yin energy to the exclusion of his yang energy.

For women, at one extreme, we have Daisy Daffodil, the doormat. Daisy exhibits yin energy to the exclusion of her yang energy.

At the other extreme, we have Bertha Balls, the ball buster. Bertha exhibits yang energy to the exclusion of her yin energy.

I'm curious. Do you recognize any of these characters in your life?

The ego serves the body. The ego is made up of the mind and the will. When the ego serves the body, we connect these two energies within ourselves. We also connect these energies with others.

There's a great book by John Sanford called *The Invisible Partners* for reference. When the ego serves the soul, we're said to be ego dystonic, or inside out.

When a man operates predominantly from his feminine energy, he's said to be ego, dystonic or inside out. When a woman operates predominantly from her masculine energy, she's said to be ego dystonic or inside out.

We live in an interesting time in our evolutionary history. I will ask you if you agree that there are more men operating from their feminine energy than ever before. Also there are more women

31

operating from their masculine energy than ever before.

We all fall somewhere along a continuum. Where we are is not set in stone. We can change where we are. It's valuable to discern where we are because where we are will reflect who we attract and who we're attracted to. Opposites attract. Similars repel. Masculine energy is attracted to feminine energy and vice versa. Feminine energy men are attracted to masculine energy women and vice versa.

There's a lid for every pot. It's important to remember equality destroys intimacy. Equity enhances intimacy.

I want to take a moment to define equity in this context. Equality is dollar for dollar. Equity is value for value. I bring the wine, you light the candles.

Equality at work is fine. We're all masculine energy at work. Equality in friendship is fine as well. "What do you feel like doing?" "I don't know, what do you feel like doing?" works fine as well.

However, in intimate, romantic relationships equality destroys intimacy. Equity enhances it. When we bring together our unique qualities we create a union. We complete the circle.

BRAIN DIFFERENCES

Anatomically the brain is divided into two hemispheres. The left side is the thinking, masculine, yang energy side. The right side is the feeling, feminine, yin energy side.

The way I remember it is women are always right. It works for me, works for my wife.

The two hemispheres are connected by a bridge called the corpus callosum. The corpus callosum is smaller for right-handed men than it is for all women and left-handed men. Right-handed men tend to bifurcate. They tend to be in one lobe or the other. This is the reason that when a man is concentrating, if you attempt to interrupt him he becomes agitated. Also when a man is concentrating, if you attempt to "tell him something" he can't hear you. It doesn't register. FYI.

In contrast, all women and left-handed men have a larger corpus callosum, giving them more flexibility between the two hemispheres, feeling and thinking.

Question, trivia question. Five of the last six presidents have been left handed. Guess who wasn't? George Bush, Jr. When I think of Bill Clinton or Barack Obama I think of charming, flexible negotiators. George Bush? Not so much.

There's a great book on brain differences called *Why Men Don't Listen and Women Can't Read Maps* by Barbara and Allan Pease. In it the authors describe for how millions of years men have gone off long distances to hunt and made it back to the home base. Women tended to stay closer to the home base.

I experienced this phenomenon firsthand when I went to Taiwan with my wife. We went to visit her uncle in a neighboring city. In the morning her uncle's wife took us to breakfast. Since she was driving I didn't pay much attention to the direction we were going because I had no intention of getting out of the car. On the way back my wife decided to get out of the car to look at some sites. Confident she knew where we were and how to get back to the house, I got out.

I was wrong. Turns out she didn't know exactly where we were or how to get back to the house. Not a problem. We'll call the house. Turns out she left the cell phone at the house. Surely she knows the address, we'll take a taxi. Not so.

Relying on my ancient wisdom I remembered we travelled east to get to the restaurant. I decided to head west. I recognized a few landmarks, headed a bit south. Obviously we made it back because I'm here to tell the tale. However, our brains are different.

I can also verify that men use 2000 words a day, women use 5000.

The left hemisphere, the masculine yang energy side, is concerned with thinking. The right side, the feminine yin energy side, is concerned with feeling. The left side is at home in the mind; the right side in the body. The left side is concerned with money; the right side sensual and sexual.

There's a great book by Leonard Shlain called *Sex, Time and Power*. In it he describes how for millions of years men have brought resources, primarily meat, to the relationship. Woman have brought fertility and beauty.

The left side says pain is okay. The right side says no to pain. The right side is the home of the limbic brain. The limbic brain is 2 to 4 million years old. It's a non-talk center. It communicates through tones, gestures, postures and facial expressions which make up 85 percent of communication. It communicates through intimidation or seduction.

The left side is the home of the neocortical. The neocortical is 44,000 years old. It's a talk center. It communicates through words, signs and symbols which make up 15 percent of communication. It communicates through negotiation. This is an important point. Consider it a landmark which we'll go over in more detail at a later time.

For now, remember our brains are different. As the French say "vive la difference". Long live the difference.

YIN/YANG ENERGY IN ACTION

Chemically, hormonally, yang energy is driven by testosterone. It affects the brain, it affects the body. Yin energy is driven by estrogen. It affects the brain, it affects the body.

Yang energy is driven to be active, it is driven to compete, control or conquer. Yin energy is driven to be passive, magnetic. It is driven to be passive, patient, vulnerable .

Generally men like their mantra. Compete, control, conquer. Not a problem Women often have to say their mantra through gritted teeth. Passive, patient, vulnerable. Often they have to add a line, passive, patient, all men are idiots, vulnerable.

These are the two mantras. I want to break down these two mantras word by word, starting with the word, **compete**.

Men are driven to compete with each other. They're not driven to compete with women. Men compete with each other because when they win, their testosterone levels go up. When they lose, they go down. You can see these extremes in professional athletes.

Men aren't driven to compete with women because it doesn't have the same effect. When men and women compete with each other, they fight, it's draining. Men want to compete for women, not against them. It brings out the best in them.

Women win by being passive, magnetic. They get what they want by knowing what they don't want. For example: They let men show their cards. A man says, "You're so hot. Let's have sex." "No." "You're the sexiest thing I've ever seen." She says, "No." "Why not, come on, let's have sex." "No.".

Men fall in love with their eyes. Women fall in love with their ears. Women listen to the deal. What are they listening for? Integrity. They are listening for a man who has a plan for the two of them. Men win by competing. "I'm the best." Women win by being passive. "Great. You're the best. Show me the deal."

Second word: **Conquer**. I didn't say, rape or pillage, I said, conquer, to win over. The essence of courtship.

Men are driven to conquer. It's in men's DNA to conquer. Each other, themselves. And especially women. Real women recognize this energy and use Aikido. They don't attempt to conquer back. By being patient, they transform this energy in a way that works for them. Patience is incredibly potent. It transforms the impossible.

Men and women in relationships are often described as impossible.

Women allow men to conquer them. Real men surrender their sword to a woman who knows how to sidestep their fight with the art of patience. It's no accident, patience is a virtue because patience conquers all.

Men marry virtue. Women marry integrity.

Control: By control, I don't mean "Tell me what to do." I mean control. To lead, to have a plan of action.

Men are driven to control. This is often a sticky point. I hear women say, "He's so controlling." I hope that he is. I hope he has a plan for you.

Men "control" the women they want to be with. They do it for, among other reasons, to insure their progeny are theirs. Women allow men to control.

It's an illusion. Women express their feminine energy by being vulnerable. It's an incredible turn on. Women, by nature, are gigantic orgasmatrons. Everything they touch, taste, see, smell or hear turns them on or off. Women feel good to do good. Men do good to feel good. When a man can "control", his testosterone levels go up. When a woman can be vulnerable, her estrogen levels go up. It's a hormonal party for everyone.

Courting is a game we give up parts of ourselves to play. The irony is there's no man as strong, as in control as a woman inside. Conversely, there's no woman as sensitive, as vulnerable, as a man inside.

We don't technically need each other. We want each other. We play the game of courtship like everyone else in the animal kingdom as an act of love.

First men's mantra: Compete, control, conquer.

Women's mantra: Passive, patient, vulnerable.

YIN/YANG
Part 2

ENERGY IN ACTION

The second mantra for yang energy is give, protect, cherish. What is it? Give, protect, cherish. The second mantra for yin energy is receive, be available, respect. What is it? Receive, be available, respect.

I want to break down this second mantra starting with the word **give**.

Men in action give. They give concretely. For example, they take a woman to dinner. Women receive. That's it. They then give back abstractly. They show appreciation. They give consent to court. You can see this throughout the animal kingdom. Typically the male brings a gift. Usually food. The female receives. She doesn't go out and bring him back something to eat. That would be equality. Equality in romantic relationships destroys intimacy. Men give concretely. Women receive, give back abstractly. "Thank you."

Men fall in love when they give. Women fall in love when they receive.

Second word, **protect**.

Men in action protect. They protect what's important to them. If they're real men, they protect women, children, animals and the planet. If they're not real men, they protect themselves. They abuse women, children, animals and the planet.

Women allow men the honor of protecting them by being available. You can't protect something that isn't there. Men show protection by leading, by creating a plan of action.

For example, a leading man will design a date. "We'll go out for dinner on Friday. I'll pick you up at 7:00. We'll go out for Chinese food. How do you feel about that?"

Unless she's deathly allergic to Chinese food, feminine energy will be available to this plan. Unless his request is unethical or immoral, she'll follow this plan.

Lead and follow. One Fred, one Ginger. Two Freds is a slam dance. Two Gingers is a disco. One Fred, one Ginger, it's a waltz.

When a woman is available to follow, she won't immediately change the plan and take control. For example, she won't say, "Friday. No Friday. Next week. I'll call you next week." Or, "7:00. No. 7:30 works better for me." Or, "Chinese food? No. Chinese food, I'm on a diet. I'm only eating Italian." You get my point.

Men show protection by leading, by creating a plan of action. Women show availability by following.

Third word: **Cherish**. The real magic of women is that women want to be cherished for their feelings. This is what makes women enigmatic to men. It's the depth of their feelings, their inner strength, their vulnerability, that magnetizes men in polarity. Opposites attract.

People ask, "What's cherishing?" Cherishing is loving the unlovable. It's loving a baby before its bath. It's easy to love a baby after its bath. Cherishing is loving a baby before its bath. In poopy pants. I have a pledge. A Dr. Pat Allen pledge. For all the men in the room, who want their stock to go way up with all the women in the room and all the women on the planet. If you're such a man, raise your right hand and repeat after me: "I promise, on my honor, to give, protect and cherish women, children, animals and the planet even when they're irrational, illogical and often irritating. So help me, God."

This is cherishing.

Last word: Respect. Men want to be respected. Respected for their thinking. When a man is respected, it's heaven for him. Men go after sex; however, they crave respect, they thrive on it. Having a woman to cherish gives a man drive, direction. Men do good to feel good; women feel good to do good.

When a man is respected, his eyes light up, he feels cherished. When a women is cherished, her heart opens up. She feels respected. We mirror each other. I have a pledge. A Dr. Pat Allen pledge for all the women in the room who want their stock to go way up with all the men in the room and all the men on the planet. If you're such a woman, raise your right hand and repeat after me: "I promise, on my honor, to respect the man I'm with even when I know I'm smarter and can do it better if I wanted to. So help me, God."

This is respect.

The second Men's Mantra: Give, protect, cherish.

The second Women's Mantra: Receive, be available, respect.

Yang energy gives, protects and cherishes. The Yin energy that receives is available and respects. Yin energy receives, is available and respects the Yang energy that gives, protects and cherishes.

INTENTION

Yang energy is expressed through the vehicle of the male body. Maleness. We're all a mixture of yin and yang energy; however, we see beauty in our reflective counterparts. Yin energy is expressed through the vehicle of the female body. Femaleness. Yang energy is at home in the mind being mentally well. Yang energy uses intuition. It intuits from bits of data to know.

When a man is mentally well, his desires for money and sex will be balanced. When a man is not mentally well, i.e., not loving others first, i.e., not loving women, children, animals and the planet first, his desires for money and sex become out of balanced obsessions.

Yin energy is at home in the body being physically well. Yin energy uses instinct to know. It feels through the senses to know. When a women is physically well, her desires for relationships will be balanced. When a woman is not physically well, i.e., not loving herself first, i.e., not saying no to what is immoral or unethical, her relationships become out of balanced obsessions.

KEYWORDS TO NEGOTIATE

I teach androgynous semantic realignment, the doctorial work of my beloved mentor, Dr. Pat Allen. Androgynous means we're all a mixture of yin and yang energy. Semantic is the use of words. Realignment means to realign how we use words and language to communicate our wants and our don't wants with others.

Words create dynamic magnetism in relationships. Feminine energy is magnetic. Masculine energy is dynamic. Words reflect how energy circulates, how it becomes synergistic in healthy, intimate relationships.

1. Yang energy gives concretely. Yin energy receives and gives back abstractly through appreciation.

2. Yang energy is about action, performance. It is the performer. Yin energy is receptive, it observes, it processes. It is the processor. Yang energy is concerned primarily with thinking. Yin energy is concerned primarily with feeling. Yang energy wants to be respected for its thinking. Yin energy wants to be cherished for its feeling. Yang energy in action is the leader. It initiates action. Yin energy is the follower. This is beautifully experienced in partner dancing.

Yang energy is the asserter. It's the call to action. Yin energy is the responder, the one who answers the call. It's call and response. Yang energy is the protector. Yin energy the protected. Yang energy is the provider. Men do good to feel good. Yin energy is the provided. Women feel good to do good. Yang energy is active. Yin energy is passive, magnetic.

Yang energy has the ability to love others first, to put the needs of women, children, animals and the planet above his own. Yin energy is self-love. Yin energy must love self first to be in integrity, to be virtuous. Yin energy is experienced in the body. Yang energy in the mind.

COURTSHIP VERSUS
EMOTIONAL DATING

Courtship flows in a circular, replenishing flow. Directionally it looks like this. Masculine energy gives concretely. Feminine energy receives, gives back abstractly. It's synergistic, giving, receiving.

In emotional dating the energy flows in the opposite direction. Women give concretely, for example, money and sex to please men who receive what they know they haven't earned and have no right to have. They end up using and abusing, leaving the man feeling guilty and the woman feeling angry.

AMIGO TALK

Feminine yin energy wants to be cherished for its feelings. Masculine yang energy wants to be respected for its thinking. These preferences are not gender bound. In fact, the last place you can tell where someone is coming from nowadays is gender. The questions to ask are: "Do I want my feelings cherished more than I want my thoughts respected? Or do I want my thoughts respected more than my feelings cherished? Or do I want both?"

Wanting both is narcissistic, which is perfectly healthy for single people. If you want both, stay single.

I want to talk about how to talk in a way that enhances this dynamic. It's called Amigo Talk. This is the invention of my beloved teacher, Dr. Pat Allen.

Simply put, if you have decided to be the yin energy, don't ask how yang energy feels about things. Do ask for thoughts, wants, opinions, ideas and suggestions. Once you receive an answer, then ask what you can do to help yang energy do whatever is desired.

If you've decided to be the yang energy, don't ask yin energy for thoughts, opinions, ideas or suggestions. Do ask for feelings. Then ask how you can help you and "her" feel better.

Simply, the yin energy, the right lobe, the cherished one, says to the yang energy, the left lobe, "What do you think?" Then the yin energy says, "What can I do to help you do it?" The yang energy, the left lobe, the respected one, says to the yin energy, "How do you feel? What can I do to help you feel better?"

SWITCHING ROLES

If you as the yang energy have feelings you want to share, which you will, first signal and get permission. For example, "Honey, I have some uncomfortable feelings I want to share with you. When is it comfortable for you to hear them today?"

If you're the yin energy and have a thought, opinion, idea or suggestion, which you will, first signal by asking for permission. For example, "Honey, I have a thought, idea, opinion, suggestion. When is it convenient for you to hear it today?"

Or in the short form, "Honey, I have a suggestion, do you want to hear it?"

These tools may seem mechanical, even archaic; however, they work. Try them. These tools rewire the brain; words, language rewire the brain. If you want to change or enhance your current dynamic use these tools.

My teacher Dr. Pat Allen's book *Getting to I Do* is a must read. This is but a brief interpretation.

PART III – STORIES

FIXER UPPERS

All men are fixer uppers. They don't come fully assembled. They're a combination of what they learn from their mother and all the women who've come before you. The learning curve for men and women is entirely different.

For women it's an actual curve. For men it's more of a straight line with a slight rise at the end of it. Usually at the end of the relationship, right around the time you say I'm done.

The time when he says, "I'm so sorry, I messed up. Can we get back together?" You say, "I'm done." He asks, "Why?" You say, "You don't have the feeling anymore." Or as my wife says, "You killed my feeling." Men are slow learners.

How many people do any kind of partner dancing, ballroom, waltz, tango, salsa? I met my wife dancing salsa. Partner dancing is a great example of the learning curve between men and women. When a woman first starts learning she catches on quickly. If she's with a good leader he can make her look really good very easily. She says, "Wow, I'm pretty good."

For men it's entirely different. When a man starts learning it's painful. Maybe because we're left brain and can do only one thing at a time. It's painful to watch. If he dances with a good woman follower she's no help. In fact, if she's not patient she'll look at him like he's an idiot. However, if a man persists, after a while he'll have what's called a growth spurt. After being terrible for months he'll suddenly be a good leader.

As men we remember the women who were patient with us in the beginning and the ones who weren't. It's the same in relationships. It's analogous to this work. I ask women how they're doing in their dating and they say, "Okay. But the guy asked me what I think and told me how he feels. I'm not seeing him anymore."

I suggest to them that they be patient, that the learning curve is much different for men. I also say that it's a tremendous gift when anyone is willing to be intimate with us for any length of time. And it's an honor when people are willing to duke it out with us. In essence, be patient. All men are fixer uppers.

FILL IN THE OTHER 23 HOURS, THEN HAVE SEX

A lot of deals I hear hinge around sex. I say they don't. If you haven't had sex for a while, sex seems like the deal. However, it's not. I suggest filling in the other 23 hours, then have sex. Start with in what my opinion is the No. 1 thing. Someone you can laugh with, someone you can spend hours and hours with, someone whose company you enjoy.

Then sex will weave seamlessly into your relationship because when you're done you won't feel empty. You will have already filled out the other 23 hours.

The times I've felt empty after sex, and there have been many, invariably there was a gap, a hole in the relationship. It was based on goal oriented sex. When often, if I had taken sex out of the equation, I wouldn't even want to spend the other 23 hours with the person.

My suggestion is to fill in the other 23 hours first, then have sex.

THE PROMISE RING

To me, the Promise Ring is overrated. My wife is from Taiwan. In Taiwan there's no such thing as a Promise Ring.

If I could have sex with a woman by giving her a Promise Ring, I would do it. It's like leasing a car. You get a new car, you have the option to buy, and you take the car off the market. How many people have had someone say, "I won't do it again. I promise." I rest my case.

A ring is a symbol of a relationship you already have. A ring will not give you a relationship.

Are we aware that guys will promise anything to have sex with you? A ring. That's easy. I suggest working on the other 23 hours.

We talk about waiting a year before marrying. Getting to know someone in every season. I say, this is good advice.

I also suggest we get to know someone for all 24 hours of the day. Sleep next to someone—not sleep with them, next to them. Snuggle, kiss, whatever, but sleep. Ask yourself, "Do I sleep better with this person? Does my body feel safe or am I just exhausted from sex and I'll leave in the morning?"

Make is seamless. I knew I wanted to be with my wife very early on. My actions showed it. I don't believe in promises. I believe in agreements. A relationship is built on a series of agreements. If I tell my wife I'll call her tomorrow, I do. I say, we'll go out on Friday, we do. I tell her I'll go to Taiwan, I go.

She tells me she'll come back in two months, she does.

A ring is a symbol of a long list of kept agreements, an unbroken circle, a chain of events that keeps going. I'm with my wife today because we keep agreeing to do more. We agree to come home, to go dancing, to go to breakfast, to go to dinner. We agree to fill in the other 23 hours, not for the goal of having sex, rather because we enjoy those hours together.

People say to me, "James, that's great, but how about the sex?" What kind of sex are we talking about? I'm talking about the kind of sex where I can devour my wife with full masculine energy, a sex she can surrender into with total feminine energy. Agreement makes for amazing sex. It gives you the freedom to be yourself.

What are the things we negotiate up front?

There are three things. Monogamy, continuity and longevity. I call that 24 hours, one day at a time. If you can string together 24 hours, you'll have continuity. If you can string these days together, you'll have longevity. If you fill in the other 23 hours, you'll have monogamy.

FAIR MARKET VALUE

In David Buss's book *The Evolution of Desire* he describes how men bring status and security, i.e., resources to a relationship. Women bring fertility and beauty in which I have interjected the term fair market value.

If I were to assess my fair market value I would say I was of average physicality, average status and security, i.e., resources. However, if I decide I only want to date super models it might be a little lean for me in the dating pool. As a man I can raise my value by working hard to obtain more resources or I could lower my expectations about needing a super model until somewhere in between I would have a match.

Women have a much different graph. They start out high with fertility and beauty. However, they're time sensitive. Their best deals are often early. Often times things happen and this one didn't work out. The guy left, he was a jerk, etc. Until, for example, she's about mid-range, let's say 40. Now she could go with a 20-year-old because these men typically don't have a lot of status and resources. Or she could go with a man 10 to 15 years older, say 50 or 55. For him a woman who's 40 is youthful. It's all relative.

My point is that it's immensely helpful to determine your fair market value at any given time.

My mom is 70; she looks good for 70, with a lot of energy. She lives in a senior home. When I visit her she says all these guys are hitting on her. She points out those two over there are hooking up. That guy is a Romeo. He hits on all the girls. She's with him because he has cigarettes.

It's interesting to note that it doesn't end, that there's a lid for every pot.

ALPHA VERSUS BETA

Alphas are complicated people. They can think and feel at any given moment. They're fully self-actualized and individuated.

You know who else is fully actualized and individuated? Narcissists. They often do best alone.

My wife, bless her, is a beta. Thank God she's a beta. Betas are simple people. For example, my wife likes to eat. When I eat, I eat for nutritional value. I eat for optimal fuel for mind and body. My wife eats because it tastes good. I say, "Tastes good? Your food has no nutritional value, it's junk." She says it makes her happy. I ask, "Happy?" She says, "Yes, happy. You eat all that nutritional food but you're always grumpy." Good point.

I also work with betas. Betas aren't concerned with being altruistic. They're not asking themselves if they're fulfilling their life's purpose. No. They only care about making money. They, by their own accounts, say they're happy. They too ask me, "James, how come you're always grumpy?"

I've decided to consciously fake beta. I've decided to act like a beta. I cherish my wife and take care of her. I appreciate that she respects me. And for the first time in my life I feel grounded, I feel happy. Don't get me wrong, I still like alpha. I still hang out with alphas. I'm still attracted to alphas.

However, I've consciously decided to fake beta, to fake it until I make it; to act as if until the feelings follow. For the first time in my life I feel at home, at peace.

IDEAS TO INCREASE YANG ENERGY

One. Do Krav Maga, an Israeli self defense system. By striking and kicking, absorbing punches and kicks you desensitize yourself from pain. Pain is okay. It also teaches how to be aggressive immediately to increase power and conviction. The ability to fight is ancient wisdom inherited in men. It promotes camaraderie among men.

Two. Work. Produce. Make money. Men do good to feel good. Being productive produces testosterone and self-esteem. Keys to yang energy.

Three. Eat red meat. Protein builds strength, maintains drive and aggression, keeps the brain alert. It creates a hunger for life energetically.

Four. Learn to partner dance. Learn to lead. It will give you experience in directing women. As a bonus you'll touch a variety of women. Being close, touching, touch and smell are the beginnings of chemistry.

Five. Lift weights. Pushing and pulling against external forces enhances your physical strength and fortitude.

Six. Do Hatha Yoga to balance your yin and yang energy and maintain flexibility. Ha means sun, Tha means moon. Hatha Yoga balances these energies within yourself.

Seven. Love. Love brings out the best in you.

IDEAS TO INCREASE YIN ENERGY

One. Work easy. Long hours of work depletes yin energy. If you must, find ways to unwind.

Two. Be social. Have lots of female friends.

Three. Social dance, partner dance. Learning to follow increases receptivity while experiencing differences in how men lead.

Four. Take time to unwind after work, take a bath, listen to music, dance or do light yoga classes.

Five. Change clothes after work. Wear dresses, jewelry, dress up like you were when you were a little girl.

Six. Remember your inner girl, your fun free child and celebrate her.

Seven. Remember women feel good to do good. Do things that feel good, i.e., eat your favorite foods. Avoid dieting, do what feels good.

Eight. Flirt. Eye contact and smile. Wait for a man to speak first. He who speaks first is masculine.

Nine. Say no to free sex. Uncommitted sex is masculine.

Ten. Love. Love yourself first.

PART IV – COMMUNICATION

HOW TO CONFRONT RATIONALLY

I want to speak about how to confront rationally as opposed to emotionally. They start out the same way. For example, let's say someone suddenly comes up to you and says, "You're a jerk." First you'll sense it in your body, typically in your stomach or the center of your chest or throat. Second, if you're acting emotionally you'll immediately react, i.e., yelling back or even hitting the person.

Then you'll think about it after, usually regrettably, i.e., why did I hit him? Now I'm in jail. The reason you're in jail is because you reacted emotionally. You went in this direction. You went feel, react, think later. What did you do? You went feel, react, think about it later. This is the essence of emotional confrontation.

Rational confrontation starts out the same way, i.e., someone suddenly yells at you, "You're a jerk." Again, you sense it viscerally in the body, in the gut, somewhere. However, instead of immediately reacting this time you take the time to translate the sensation into a feeling. You now feel angry, hurt, sad, etc. At that point you take the feeling up to your thinking where you decide how you want to act. You weigh out the price and the prize first.

For example, you may still want to hit the person, an enjoyable prize; however, you may not be willing to pay the price of going to jail. Having weighed out the price and the prize you then decide to act in your own best interests. This is rational confrontation. It's feel, think, act. Feel, think, act.

STROKE AND STAND

Let's say you're in a more intimate situation, for
example, a first date. Let's say you're a woman.
The date's going well, you're talking, getting along,
etc., when suddenly the guy wants to have sex with
you. If you react emotionally you may hit the guy,
leave or yell at the guy, saying, "Are you crazy? I
don't even know you." You would feel, react, think
about it later, often regrettably. Sometimes not.

However, let's say that today is this guy's lucky
day. No, it's not what you're thinking. Today
you've decided to act rationally. There's a tool
called the stroke and stand. No, it's not what you're
thinking. The stroke and stand is made up of three
parts. There are two basic needs that everyone has:
to be heard and known.

We use this in the stroke. For example: "I
appreciate your wanting to have sex with me. You
have every right to ask me to have sex with you."
This is a stroke. We make the person right, even if
we think they're wrong.

Now comes the stand, speaking as a woman:
"However, I feel I don't want to have sex with you
until I get to know you better." This is the stand.

Now comes the contract. "Will you cherish me and
wait until I know you better?"

At this point you'll learn some very important information about the person. If they agree, if they have the ability to put your feelings first, you'll learn it now. However, let's say in the heat of the moment it didn't register and they continue to ask you to have sex as if that never happened.

Then we have what's called a second stroke and stand. The second stroke and stand comes with a price tag. For example: "I appreciate that you want to have sex with me and you keep asking me." Stroke. "However, I feel I don't want to have sex with you until I get to know you better and don't want to talk about this further." Stand. The price for continuing to ask me to have sex is I'll leave, not talk to you, whatever you feel the price should be.

We only do two stroke and stands. More than that leads to uproar.

You may say, "Wow, James, that's great. Where were you when I needed you last week?" Good question.

Let's say some time has passed. You didn't address the situation in the moment that it happened and now you have a feeling. For example, you're mad. Then we can do what's called a five-step cleanup. It's a stroke and stand with two other steps.

First, time has passed. Now you'll want to signal the person first rather than immediately and emotionally react to them the next time you see them. For example, first signal them. "I have some uncomfortable feelings I want to talk to you about regarding our date last week. When would it be convenient for you to hear them today?" That's a signal. It prepares the person to hear what you have to say.

Let's say he says, "Now is fine." Remember, use the stroke first. "I appreciate that you wanted to have sex with me and you had every right to ask me." Remember you haven't said any of this before so this is the first time. "However, I feel I don't want to have sex with you until I know you better. Will you cherish me and wait until I know you better?"

The real question here is not what's right or wrong. It's finding out if your feelings will be cherished if you're a woman. And if your thinking will be respected if you're a man.

This same template is used if this was a man making this stand. But he would change it from "I feel, I don't want" to "I think, I want". For example: "However, I *think* I *want* to wait until I know you better to have sex with you." A very hypothetical example for a man.

The last tool is called validation. This is used when you're getting the silent treatment. For example, nothing is being directly said; however, you sense from the tone of their voice, their postures, gestures or facial expressions that the person is upset, angry, sad, etc. You use validation by saying, "I sense from the tone of your voice, your gestures, postures or facial expressions that you're angry, sad, hurt..." whatever you think they are. Question, "Am I right?"

You invite them to bring it up to the verbal, at which point they may say yes and begin to talk about what's bothering them. Or they may say no. You can acknowledge them and say, "If you ever do want to talk about it, feel free."

This is validation.

10 WAYS TO SPEAK RATIONALLY

There are 10 key emotional phrases that when removed from your speech will dramatically change your life. Most of these phrases we've learned are "polite." Being polite is often a way of not being potent, of not saying what we want or don't want in a direct way.

The use of the antidote to these emotional phrases will result in your being able to say and ask for what you want and don't want in a direct, cherishing and respectful way.

One. Remove I should, you should, ought to, must, have to. Remove those phrases. Doing what you should do, ought to, must do, have to is a great way to ruin your body chemistry. It produces cortisol which ruins your immune system over time. It's not a potent way to speak. The remedy is to simply say I want, I don't want or I want you to.

Two. Remove I can't. I can't is another disempowering phrase often used to be evasive. Replace it with I want to or I don't want to, I will or I won't.

Three. I would like or I wish is fine for fanaticizing about an imaginary future. For example, I would like to go to France some day. It's disempowering in everyday language, i.e., I would like to talk to you. Sounds polite. If you're used to saying this it will be uncomfortable. For a while you may even feel downright demanding. Do it anyway. Change I would like to I want or I don't want.

Four. I will try is also not potent. I tried, past tense, is fine. Most people use I will try as a way of being evasive when they will not commit to doing something at a specific time or date. Change I will try to I will or I won't do it unless.

Five. May I or can I. We often learn these as children. "May I leave the table?" Again, disempowering. We can be polite and potent by changing the sentence structure. I want to leave the table. May I?

Six. Would it be all right? Would you mind? Would you like? Could we? We have so many ways of being indirect built into our language under the disguise of being polite. Again, it will be uncomfortable for a while, however change it. Simply say in all of these cases I want. Fill in the blank. Do you want? Fill in the blank.

Seven. I need. We need food, air, water and shelter, strokes positive or negative, attention positive or negative attention. Everything else is a want. Replace I need with I want.

Eight. Why? Why when used to defend thoughts, actions or feelings is also indirect language. Use why for facts, such as why are the lights on? Otherwise replace why with what are your reasons?

Nine. I'm sorry or I apologize. Unless you did something deliberately, replace this with I made a mistake and don't want to do it again. Then you can say excuse me or pardon me.

Ten. I feel that. There's no such feeling as that. Replace with I feel sad, mad, happy, jealous, etc., or I think that.

Most if not all emotional phrases are taught to us in childhood. They wire our brains. By using these alternatives we can rewire our brains to speak potently and rationally. Speaking of childhood...

EMOTIONAL VERSUS RATIONAL PARENTING

In a rational home a fun free child will say I want or I don't want because I am me. A rational, nurturing parent will say you should or should not because you will be better. The parent will present the price or the prize to the child, i.e., if you only eat chocolate all the time you will get sick. Teach the child to make adult decisions, i.e., I will or I will not based on the price and the prize for doing it.

In contrast, in an emotional home an adapted child will say I should or I should not because I am afraid, guilty, mad or sad. The emotional, critical or super parent will say you should or should not because I say so, teaching the child to make emotionally reactional decisions based on feeling and indirect unpredictable game playing.

FIRE TO WIRE THE BRAIN

Who we are plays out in the first three years of life.

In the first year of life we learn to say I want. If we're nurtured we learn to say I want my way. If we're discounted and intimidated we learn I should want it your way.

I want my way is the beginning of a potent life. I should want your way is the beginning of being impotent. Shoulds bottle up your energy. When you're discounted by yourself or others, not allowed to say or do what you want, you lose energy. We ruin the chemistry in the body, damaging the immune system, overloading the body with cortisol, priming it for dysfunction and addictions. The remedy is to say I want, not I should.

What do healthy children learn to say in the second year of life? No. A nurtured child has permission to say no, I don't want to do it your way. This is healthy. When a child is taught I should not do it my way, problems begin. This is the beginning of not trusting ourselves, not loving one's self. We lose energy by being discounted. We get bottled up issues.

In the first three years of life we learn one of either of two things. Either I learn to love me or I learn not to love me.

The remedy for the second year of life is to be able to say no.

It's in the third year of life that we learn to communicate with each other in one of three ways, either through intimidation or seduction or negotiation. You can see this on any playground. Already little kids have learned a style. Some intimidate with power. Give me that toy or I'll hit you. Or seduce you with guilt. I will give you my cookies if you'll play with me.

There are also the little negotiators. I'll let you play with my toy if you let me play with yours. These styles don't end on the playground; they continue in adult life.

A lifetime of intimidation and seduction by self and others robs us of energy, shortening our lives, ruining our health chemically from the inside. Healthy people live long lives because they negotiate win/win situations. They care about themselves and others. Being able to negotiate sets the foundation for us to be able to love others.

The remedy. To free your energy to be able to say yes to what you want, no to what you don't want and negotiate. It's simple but it's not easy.

This won't only change your romantic relationships, it will change your whole life, every relationship you have, especially your relationship to yourself.

This is the way to rewire the brain, to change the direction of your energy.

We have four natural, God-given permissions in life: to be able to be, to feel, to think and to share. This is the much talked about authentic self. There are many ways to go about it. I suggest this one. Say yes to what you want, say no to what you don't want and negotiate with others.

AGES THREE – NINE – FIFTEEN - PLUS

From the ages three to nine we observe. We observe one of two lessons. Nurtured, we learn it's safe. We learn I want to be human my way. When it's not safe, we learn I should be a human your way. Nurturing parents say you should do it because it will be best for you, explaining the price and the prize of your actions. Critical parents say you should be a human my way because I say so. We make our way back to ourselves by saying I want or I don't want to regain our humanity.

From the age of nine to 15 we learn either I want to be a sexual human being my way or I should be a sexual human being your way. This is where our relationship problems begin to manifest. Being yourself is a full time job. How we learn to be sexual is pivotal.

After 15 if we're safe and secure we say I want to be a committable, sexual human my way. If not we feel compelled to do it your way. I should be a committable sexual human being your way.

This is where we pay the price. If we have been supported and nurtured we love. If not we're susceptible to obsessions and addictions.

Being a committed sexual human being someone else's way is extremely painful and discounting. It's a half-lived life.

All of these shoulds lead to a half-lived life. The remedy is I want my way or I don't want my way. When this happens I learn to love me and in return I learn to love you.

WHAT IS INTIMACY?

If I come from an I'm okay, you're okay life position, then from zero to five I love me. From six years onward I love you. If I come from an okay you position and you do the same, we're capable of intimacy.

If I come from an I'm not okay me position I'll question do I love me? I'll question do I love me from zero to five years of age. From six onward I question do I love you? If you come from a not okay position you'll do the same. This leads to game playing.

One of the keys to normal relatedness between five and 10 years old is having a mother who respects a boy for his intelligence. The father supports and agrees. Mothers must wean their sons to make their own decisions and actions. For girls between the ages of five and 10, for normal relatedness a father cherishes a girl's feelings and the mother agrees. The father teaches the girl it's safe to feel, to be vulnerable.

If a mother disrespects a boy's intelligence from five to 10 years of age it results in pain. It could create confusion of roles in acquiring status, financial security, sensuousness and sexuality in later life, often leading to bouts of instant gratification. If a father is non-cherishing of a girl's feelings from five to 10 years of age it results in pain. It manifests as a need to control in the areas of financial security, sensuousness and sexuality.

EMOTIONAL VERSUS RATIONAL MANIPULATION

Emotional people operate unconsciously from their game of shoulds and should nots generated by fears of rejection and abandonment at the conscious level. This manifests at the social level by their attempts to intimidate/seduce themselves and others.

In contrast, rational people operate unconsciously from their wants and not wants, positive emotions and self-loving feelings at the conscious level. These manifest at the social level as the ability to negotiate with self and others.

HEDONISM VERSUS STOICISM

Hedonists are of the world. They're driven by power—power over others. Their goals are money and sex gratification, preferably instant gratification.

Stoics are in the world. They're driven by potency—potency within themselves. Their goals are physical, mental and emotional satisfaction, preferably long-term satisfaction.

Hedonists prefer power expressed as me over you. They come from a place of I. They use intimidation and seduction. They also come from a place of you don't want because I say so. Hedonism is expressed through power, me feeling good about being feared by you. It uses intimidation and seduction.

Stoics prefer potency expressed as you caring about me. They come from a place of we. We negotiate our wants and don't wants with each other.

Stoicism is expressed by me feeling good about you and me feeling good. Hedonism is promoted by negative emotions: fear, anger, guilt, shame, jealousy and depression. It's the home of the seven deadly sins: pride, coveting, lust, anger, gluttony, envy and sloth.

Stoicism is promoted by positive emotions. It has a short list. Happiness, love, joy, faith, empathy and peace.

Hedonism is promoted by despair. It's driven by the mantra of having hope for a cure for pain, physical or emotional, that's never delivered by family, church or therapy. It's the longing exemplified by the downward spiral of norepinephrine.

Stoicism is promoted by hope. It's driven by hope for a cure to be delivered. It's exemplified by the homeostatic well being of serotonin.

The effect of hedonism is a lack of dopamine and over-stimulation of adrenaline converting into cortisol, ruining the body's immune system.

The effect of stoicism is dopamine delivered to the limbic brain, the right lobe, giving the body a sense of well being.

DRIVERS VERSUS ALLOWERS

Drivers and allowers are the work of Dr. Taibi Kahler. The drivers are of the world of hedonism. Drivers ruin your immune system by stripping your nerves and damaging the body from the inside out by producing cortisol.

The first driver is "be perfect," an impossible standard for which satisfaction can't be experienced. It drives you towards constant gratification. The antidote is to be in the world, stoicism. Using the five allowers. The antidote for being perfect is "be excellent". Be excellent allows for satisfaction with doing your best always. It's attainable.

The second driver is "try harder". If you have one, get two. If you have two, get three. Again, the driver is based on a lack of satisfaction. It's the treadmill that keeps pushing your way of life. The antidote, the allower is "enough". Know what's enough. It's based in gratitude. Physical, mental and emotional satisfaction come first. A balanced life.

The third driver is "hurry up", similar to try harder. Hurry up is if you can start at 8:00, start at 7:00. Keep pushing yourself. Use every minute. Make yourself super busy, constantly going at full speed on adrenaline.

Adrenaline is designed for short bursts. When it's going constantly it becomes cortisol, which ruins the body chemistry. The antidote is "work easy" similar to enough. It's being balanced, pacing yourself, scheduling your day so you can breathe, taking the long view approach, the turtle and the hare story.

The fourth driver is "please others first". This one is often misunderstood. It's basically living by other people's standards. It's doing what you believe you should do to be accepted, liked and loved. It comes from outside one's self, wanting validation and gratification from others.

The antidote is "please self first", often misunderstood as being selfish. Please self first is self-regulated. Internal satisfaction with self and life. It comes from the position I do for me for you. The reward is in the doing for you, not in the validation or gratification received from others. Please self first is an internal compass steering from a sense of self. It's self-love, a requirement for the ability to love others.

The fifth driver is "be strong". It means don't be teachable, don't listen to others, do it your way. Control your environment and others. Feel good about being feared by others. It sets one's self apart.

The antidote allower is "be open". Be teachable, open to new ideas, flexible, not rigid. Be able to

86

negotiate with others. It is an open mind, open to possibilities.

The five drivers are be perfect, try harder, hurry up, please others first and be strong.

The five allowers are be excellent, enough, work easy, please self first and be open.

FOUR WAYS TO BECOME A STOIC

The first way to become a stoic is to have a support group, a group of like-minded fellows, family, friends, community, church, therapy or self-help. You can't take on a hedonist alone. If you put a hedonist in a room alone with a stoic you'll end up with two hedonists. Hedonists are powerful. Respect that power.

The second is the ritualization of verbal and non-verbal communication, semantic realignment. Basically changing your language, saying what you want and don't want clearly instead of using vague, emotional language, such as I should, I would like, I need to, I have to, etc. Ritualized language rewires the brain by using the same method your current world view was indoctrinated into you by talk, self-talk and the talk of others.

The third is to avoid hedonists or placate them. Don't engage. There will be people you can't avoid, bosses, family members, etc. It's often best to placate these people using their emotional language, i.e., I should, I would like, etc. When possible avoid hedonists. When not, go belly up.

Acquiesce. When you consciously choose to act emotionally it won't harm you. It's manipulation, a lie for love. Love of self.

The fourth is the deepening of the spiritual belief in a higher power that loves me and wishes me well. A belief the world is for, not against me, that all is for a highest good, always, no matter how it looks.

AIKIDO HEALING

In the first year of life if all goes well we learn to say I want. In the second year we learn to say no to what we don't want. In the third year of life we learn how to either intimidate through fear or seduce with guilt or negotiate.

Already at this point we've set a tone for our life position. If we've learned to intimidate or seduce we'll be gamey. Gamey people go about getting what they want or don't want without asking for it. Games are always unconscious. The book on this is *Games People Play* by Eric Berne. Also there's *The Drama Triangle* by Steve Karpman.

In *The Drama Triangle* there are three basic positions. One is the persecutor or intimidator or critical parent. Another is the rescuer or the seducer or super parent. The last position is the victim or adapted child.

There are different games for each position. For example, the persecutor plays the game blemish. I couldn't possibly go out with someone taller than me, etc., basically finding a way to discount others.

The favorite game for the rescuer is I'm only trying to help you. Again, another way of discounting people by making them appear helpless. A favorite game of the victim is kick me, a way of discounting one's self by setting other people up to abuse you.

All of these games, of which there are many more, have their payoff in positive and negative strokes. However, they're a poor substitute for intimacy.

Intimacy is the ability to negotiate. It's the ability to ask for what you want and say no to what you don't want with people you care about. This is the healing that comes from our childhood prejudice, judgments we were taught by others to be true. For example, all "fill in the blank" people are bad. Along with that are our delusions, things we made up to be true based on our limited experiences, i.e., don't climb trees on Saturday because one time you fell down from a tree on a Saturday.

It's in sorting these things out that we come back to balance. A balanced person is individuated and actualized. Individuated yang energy in that they know who they are and what they want. Actualized, yin in that they know how they feel and what they don't want.

Our healing is a return to our natural God-given state, the ability to be, feel, think and share our way. Individuated and actualized means I will be myself.

SECOND AND THIRD ORDER OF STRUCTURE

Second order of structure consists of the messages we get from outside ourselves. The basic message being you should do it my way or I'll discount you or I want to mold you. These are the outside neocortical prejudices we're taught.

From these messages we develop our own internal delusions, learned responses such as I should not do it my way or I will do it your way or I won't because I want to survive. All of these messages weigh heavy on the soul.

The antidote is simple. We were born with it. It's our third order of structure expressed as you should be you by a nurturing parent. It's expressed as I will be myself, an individuated and actualized adult. I want to be, feel, think and share my way.

TOOLS

The way out of a negative feeling is a positive decision followed by action or inaction as soon as possible.

Dip stick. If you're uncertain about a particular either/or decision you can dipstick. Take a piece of paper and write down the two alternatives. For example, move to Detroit or don't move to Detroit. Then ask yourself: if I had to make a choice in this moment which would I choose? Mark it down on one side or the other. Periodically dip stick yourself and ask again. Mark it down so you can get a reading from your unconscious.

Another form of dipstick is a blind study. Have a bag or box with two colors of paper, one for yes and one for no. Then vote by color and then count at the end of the test, i.e., after a day or after a week or after several weeks. This eliminates the influence of seeing your previous votes while you're voting.

LOSER'S LOOP

There are four signs of a loser in communication.

One. They're abrupt. They speak in one-word sentences, i.e., no, maybe, I don't know.

Two. They're evasive. They won't commit to a specific time. They say they'll do it later or soon or some day.

Three. They're secretive. They expect you to know what they want without asking for it. If they have to ask for it, it's too much trouble.

Four. They're condescending. They either talk up or talk down to you. These are the four signs of a loser.

THE WINNER'S CIRCLE

Winners in communication talk. They create win/win situations. They negotiate. They do it without using intimidation through fear or seduction with guilt. They're open minded, willing to learn. They're approachable.

Winners also can say what they want. They negotiate. They say what they want without using intimidation or guilt. They can share, compromise and work with others for solutions. Winners in communication engage with others. They don't hold themselves apart. They've learned to be an I. They can now be a we and an us. They include others, which leads to satisfaction with a loving, well-lived life. Their energy flows freely.

LOVE OR JUST SEX

Love is who you are. Sex is something you do.
Love heals the soul. Sex feeds the body. It's a
matter of depth. When I see you your body parts do
it all. Men fall in love with their eyes.

When I love I see your energy. Often men tell me
she's so hot. I ask what is she like? They say she's
so hot. Where does she live? Man, she is so hot.
What does she do? Smoking hot. Hmm, I get it.

We love projection. Anything to get us out of
ourselves—cars, clothes, shoes, people—you name
it. The challenge is people come with higher price
tags: buy now, pay later. I love instant gratification,
practiced it for many years. I just can't afford it on
the back end.

It turns out we're all energy. Energy is all there is.
We're shown love as a vortex, something we fall
into. It can take years to get out.

Sex rarely leads to love.

GETTING THE RING

Every deal is only as good as the people who make it. Getting the ring is not a goal, it's a process. You don't know a person until you see what they're like when they don't like you or don't agree with you. I hope you have this experience before you marry.

I married my wife for her integrity, her wholeness. There will always be someone hotter, younger, sexier—you name it. Love heals what already hurts in you. It's how we're seen. Until then we're projections, replaceable parts in an ongoing drama of projection.

If you don't want to be hurt or if you feel it's wrong to be hurt, don't love. Humans hurt each other. We're healed by the same poison that originally bit us. Maybe your parents, maybe your ex—someone got in deep to initiate you. Welcome to the planet.

Now what are we going to do? Make everyone else pay? That will work for a while until no one else wants to play or needs the lesson. Building a wall that keeps people out also keeps you in. I suggest get hurt, bite the snake that bit you. Hurt more until it releases you from its grip the only way it can, with surrender. It's going to get worse, I guarantee it. So what?

I heard a guy complaining that after seven months his live-in girlfriend started nagging him. He didn't sign up for that. I wanted to tell him, good news, she loves you. We only fight with people we care about. We're only real with people we care about. I wanted to ask him if there was any possibility after this much time he had started taking her for granted. He said she wasn't like that in the beginning. I don't think it occurred to him how much he had changed since the beginning. It rarely does.

We're constantly being mirrored, often not as the great people we think we are, more like the thoughtless people who leave the clothes on the floor or don't wash the dishes. Talk about bursting the romantic bubble.

I definitely need a new wife. Or maybe I'll get better at picking up clothes and washing dishes, little things other people think are important. Maybe I'll remember how attentive I was in the beginning, how much attention I gave her during courtship, because somewhere in between there's a balance, a maturity that aches to be born, to evolve, to love.

THE PLOW

It turns out it was the plow, the plow that sent us on the marital course. As hunters and gatherers we were basically equals as far as livelihood went. We could easily disband from partners and rejoin with others relatively unencumbered by needs and possessions. Left to our natural devices relationships statistically lasted three to four years, about the time it takes to get a child on his feet where he can be taken care of by the larger community.

In many ways we're coming full circle. Statistics show that as more women work and become independent divorce rates go up, a natural outgrowth of being less encumbered by need.

The plow tied us to the land. It took away a woman's job as a gatherer, creating the first unemployment crisis. Men took up food production because the plow was heavy and it was pulled by large animals. When this happened women's autonomy went with it.

As we became tied to the land it was no longer as possible to walk away and rejoin elsewhere. Need was born. Men and women needed each other.

Patriarchy was born 3000 years ago. It's meeting another crossroads today. Today in 2011 it's women who are thriving. The economic downturn has affected men much more in terms of job loss. Women are now the majority in the workforce. Nine out of the 10 top new fields for jobs are dominated by women.

They say history repeats itself. Here we go.

The question people ask is why get married? There's one difference today. We recognize we are spiritual beings having a human experience.

In my experience marriage is the most spiritual thing I've ever done. The question will be are we going around in circles or are we headed towards freedom? Only time will tell.

PART V– LOVE

INTRODUCTION

I was first introduced to my teacher, Dr. Pat Allen's work three months after I got married. I read her book *Getting to I Do* and it was everything I did. I waited a year to get married. I went through the first three months, the perfect phase. The three to six month imperfect phase. The six to nine month negotiation phase. And the nine to 12 month commitment phase.

I negotiated time, space, money and play. Got an engagement ring and a year and five months later got married. I have clinically trialed this work on myself and it works.

Another area I clinically trialed on myself is being ego dystonic, being inside-out. I had a male body with major yin energy. My father was an alcoholic, I'm left-handed, I was a singer/songwriter, musician, poet. From the age of 12 to 24 I smoked marijuana every day just to make my clinical trial as authentic as possible. Of course I dated yang energy women. It almost worked, except I had just enough male energy that we fought.

In my last yang energy relationship I hit bottom. It was so painful that I really wished I had had Pat's book. It was at this point that I began to heal my

fisher king wound, which brings me to the question:
Why get married?

WHY GET MARRIED?

We live in unprecedented times. If you're married you're now a minority. For the first time there are more single than married people. The whole country of Sweden has decided not to marry. The question has become why get married?

I'm recently married and my friends ask, "So how is it being married?" Or the unsolicited "I'm never getting married."

If they do delve a little deeper they say, "I don't want to give away half my stuff." Even when all they have is five bucks.

When experts such as Napoleon Hill, author of *Think and Grow Rich*, state, and I paraphrase, when a man is inspired and backed by a woman he accomplishes far more, far more.

Last, and shall I say least, is the classic why buy the cow when they can get the milk for free?

Here, however, they do bring up an important point. Women are the gatekeepers. They're the keepers of the moral and ethical standards of a culture. They do this with one word. That word is no; no to unethical and immoral behavior.

When a man is gifted with this "no" he rises to the occasion economically, emotionally and spiritually.

Not many of us are born in a rational home. I was born in a very emotional home. My father was an alcoholic. I was a surrogate husband to my mom. It was very emotional.

My wife, however, was born in Taiwan. It's a very rational, nuclear family-oriented culture. My wife lived at home with her family until we got married at the age of 34.

In a rational home women are cherished. They're taught they're worthy. Men are taught to protect and allow women and children to be vulnerable.

It's been my observation in America if a woman doesn't marry by the time she finishes college she's culturally sent out into the world to fend for herself. Shortly thereafter she says, "Why get married? I can take care of myself." And she does.

Women make far better men than men do! Look at our world today. When a man loses his job he stays on the couch and watches the kids. Women go out and get it done. They're far better than men, which hurts me because I care about men. Maybe because I am one and maybe because we need men.

Which brings me to another topic that's dear to me: spirituality. I've done yoga for over 20 years. I've read many spiritual books. I spent 20 years in Alanon. I've been around a lot of "spiritual" people.

In my observation spiritual people are predominantly single. Why is that? It's been my observation and experience that spiritual people are predominantly emotional people. They're raised in emotional homes where they're not taught to be, feel, think and share for themselves. They're taught what to feel, what to think, what to do consciously and unconsciously by others until there's little, if any, love left for themselves. The question they ask is why get married?

In my experience the first step we relearn, we rewire, is self-love, our natural God-given state.

The second, it's relatively easy to be spiritual by yourself. Spirituality often flies out the window the moment we relate to others intimately in intimacy.

When people ask me why get married I say, "Marriage is the most spiritual thing I've ever done, and I've done a lot of down dog." The reason, and I quote Dr. Pat Allen, and my experience is, "The only way you know you love yourself or anyone else is by the commitments you're willing to make and to keep. Not to a finite fallible human being but to the relationship."

When my wife and I were fighting in the imperfect stage we made a commitment not to give up on the relationship. If I can say anything to you personally I will say find someone who's willing to fight with you because those are the people who love you.

Be kind because we're all finite fallible human beings with an infinite capacity to love.

THE INGREDIENTS

I want to talk about "the ring." Everyone knows "the ring" is not the wedding ring—it's the holy grail of rings, the engagement ring. As a man I balked at the importance and symbolism of the ring, not to mention the expense. Actually I do want to mention the expense because it's astronomical and the ring is so small.

My wife, for the most part, a relatively easy going and negotiable person, suddenly became adamant and determined about the ring. The negotiations were hard and emotional. The hardest negotiations were with myself. How could I justify the expense? In my world it was a waste of money. It made no sense to me, especially after a hard day of work.

So we went to take a look. There's one store that all men know and fear. It's called Tiffany's. The people are very nice and the rings, which I had never paid much attention to before, are immaculately displayed, multi-faceted gems.

The look on her face as she puts on the ring is priceless. The joy that emanates from her body is palpable. The ring looks like it's made for her finger. They have amazing chemistry. The rush is intense. They also inform you that upon approved credit you can have no interest for one year!

We leave the store and head towards the car without saying anything. My brain starts to struggle as reality sets in. I have one small problem—the price. If you want to know if you really want to get married, go look for a ring. Demons I thought I might have, suddenly came to the surface. Lack of self-worth, fear of financial insecurity, fear of responsibility for another. Things I realized I had cleverly avoided until now.

People say to me, "James, wow, you got married. You must have a lot of faith." I say, "No, I have payments, I have long-term goals. I want that ring to cost me a dollar a day. It'll take me 40 years of marriage to accomplish this."

My point is get the ring. I know they're expensive and a waste of money. It's also the best investment you'll ever make. Do it for you. Trust that it will strengthen you to create more abundance in your life. Do it for her. This is an important symbol for her. Make sure she loves her ring, that it's exactly what she wants. It will make her feel loved and cherished. It will help her to remember she loves you even when you piss her off, which you will.

She'll look at that ring for the rest of her life and so will you. You'll want to remember you stepped up.

THE PARENTS

Ask her dad for permission. I know you're a grown man. Ask. Be accountable. The question will make you more certain in your decision. The more people the better. When you ask you will find out how he feels and sees his daughter. Trust me, he knows her way better than you do. You may think it's old fashioned. Do it anyway. Be accountable. Being accountable to another man for his daughter will strengthen you.

I can't stress this enough. A woman's relationship to her father directly translates to a relationship with you. If it's good she'll be able to transfer her allegiance to you. If it's not, it will be much more challenging for the both of you.

Her dad sets the tone, so listen. Where is he? Can you meet him? Is it a requirement to have his approval before you marry? Hopefully the answer is yes.

NO DAD – BAD DAD

When there has been no protection or caring, people grow up wild. If a woman hasn't experienced love and protection it will be hard to open and trust a man. Know that.

Hopefully, at least one of you has experienced being loved or has done enough work to be in self-love. Don't underestimate this before you get married.

No dad. Without the experience of a father a woman is often left spinning on her own with no ground and direction. It can be a wild ride and a matter of survival. If there's no good role model of a man in her life you may be the one who receives the pain and anger at some point.

Bad dad. Even more tragic, when pain, anger, hurt and betrayal are poured in they often pour out. Remember, survival changes the rules. Take your time. Everyone has challenges. The point is to choose challenges you can handle. Investigate these things upfront. How does she feel about her dad and her experience now? If she doesn't talk or instantly displays anger consider yourself warned.

GOOD MOM – BAD MOM – NO MOM

Good mom. A good mom is a mom who raises you to be an independent man who takes care of women and children first.

A **bad mom** keeps you a boy. Does everything for you and keeps you in your fisher king wound, unable to bond to another woman.

No mom, no role model, a man is often spinning, looking for ground, often ending up with mothering women and resenting them.

THE FISHER KING WOUND

At 12 years old I was playing basketball with my two friends and three girls we were interested in. We were pairing up when suddenly there was a car crash accident on the corner. People rushed to see it; I didn't. They came back and said it was my mom. I got her and walked her home.

The next day she was in the hospital, at which point my father OD'd on prescription drugs and he was in the hospital. As I stood there alone, I received my fisher king wound.

The fisher king wound is a moment in life, usually at ages 10 to 12, when a boy loses his innocence. The cure, as Carl Jung states and has been my experience as well, is work. Not typically creative work, but steady, money-making work.

The other beautifully described in Robert Johnson's book *He* and also my own experience is, and I quote, and I love this quote. "No son ever develops into manhood without in some way being disloyal to his mother. If he remains with her to comfort and console her, then he never gets out of his mother complex. Often the mother will do all she can to keep her son with her. One of the ways is to encourage in him the idea of being loyal to her. But if he gives into her completely, then she often finds herself with a son severely injured in his masculinity. The son must ride off and leave the mother, even if it appears to be mean, disloyal. And the mother must bear the pain."

I experienced this in my life. It was my birthday and I erupted from my mother and broke our ties. I decided to create my own family. Five days later I met my wife.

THE EX

No one wants an ex. They're expensive and the war stories are painful. Often divorced men are traumatized. They blame this trauma on marriage.

I believe the seeds may have been planted long before. That's why the work is done up front. Men marry with their eyes and pay with their hearts. Real men see energy; boys see objects.

"Falling into lust turns humans into play objects with temporary value. Falling in love takes time. It takes effort but the value is more enduring." Dr. Pat Allen.

MASCULINE WOMEN

"Masculine women do not bond. They also don't orgasm. They're too head trippy. Masculine women either have been raised masculine or they have been abused or violated so they've climbed up into their head and that's where they live. Their bodies do not relate and they will not be vulnerable." Dr. Pat Allen.

LEAD AND FOLLOW

The question to ask is: Do you want your feelings cherished more than you want your thoughts respected? If so, that's yin energy. Or do you want your thoughts respected more than your feelings cherished? That's yang energy.

Another question to ask is: Do you want to be the bread winner? That's yang energy. Or do you want to be the homemaker? That's yin energy.

The reason I ask again is that half measures avail us nothing. As a woman better you stay yang energy. Yang energy women get lots of guys. They're sexy, aggressive and they don't want anything. They're a dream come true for men in the beginning.

On the contrary, yin energy women get it. They instinctively know how to follow. They get what they want by being willing not to get it. My wife's engagement ring cost $15,525.35. You know how she got it? I don't know either. It's some kind of miracle. There's no way I can spend that much money. I have a fear of financial insecurity. By most accounts I'm considered cheap. It's impossible. You know how she did it? She appreciated what I already did for her. She was able to express through her body, tones and gestures how good she would feel if she got the ring, which inspired me to do good, to feel good.

Even more, she was willing not to get it. She patiently waited through my tirades. She vulnerably showed me how she felt. She was passively willing not to get it.

Which brings me to an important point. As men, we'll intuitively test women to see if they'll follow us even when we're unreasonable. For example, I heard a story about a guy who took a woman to Santa Barbara for the weekend. He was doing really well, paying for everything; she was very happy. When suddenly he said the three words every woman wants to hear. Let's go shopping. Now she thought she was in heaven. Of course she accepted.

While shopping she found a belt she liked. You know what he did? He said, "You should buy it, it looks great on you."

"Test." What did she do? She immediately called her single friends to get their advice and joined her in being incensed. Wouldn't you?

First. May I suggest don't call your single friends. When I went to Taiwan to get married to my wife a second time, I told my single friend. You know what he said? "I would never do that, that's ridiculous." Perhaps that's why he's single.

You know what my married friends said? "Have a good trip."

Getting back to the belt. The second thing I want to suggest, stake your game. We'll unconsciously test a woman to see if she'll take care of herself. We just met a woman and we don't want to pay all her bills right away. Who does? Later we'll think about it and feel bad and want to make it up to her. i.e., buy the belt or something else. We're testing to see if she'll jump all over us when we mess up because we know we'll mess up. We want to know how she'll handle it.

Next example. There was a very beautiful woman who expressed how a man had promised her the moon, i.e., an apartment close to him and other things she didn't mention. When suddenly, after having sex with her and before moving in, he balked. He backed out of the deal.

Suggestion. Know we'll promise anything to have sex with a woman and even mean it until the bill comes. If you're a woman, find a man whose lifestyle you're able to live with where he is now; otherwise he'll eventually resent you and break the deal.

My last example and perhaps the most important. There was a lovely girl who was in a quandary because she promised her boyfriend in Germany that he could live with her. Then instinctually felt bad about it and didn't want to do it. She was spinning and confused. You know why? Because she had no ratchet. Do you know who the ratchet is for a woman? Her dad.

I recently asked a group of women how many of them would have to ask their dad's permission to marry. No one raised their hand. It's a dad, a culture, a community, that requires a man to marry.

As my teacher so eloquently said that night, it's for your honor.

You know why I got married? It's not because I'm some great guy. It's because it was required to be with my wife. If I wanted her, I had to ask her dad. She described how he didn't like many people until I was concerned. However, I did it anyway. We weren't allowed to live together until we were married. He staked her game, i.e., he made sure she had money and a place to live until she found the right person for her.

If you have a dad, great. For many of us we'll have to stake our game and find the support of others, which is why I write this now, because I want to go to your wedding. I want to say the words to you I heard so many times at my wedding: "Congratulations. Congratulations."

THE FIGHT

It's not a matter of if, it's a matter of when. One of the ways you'll know you love someone is when you find someone who's willing to fight with you because these are the people who love you.

Each time you make it to the other side it's a building block. Commit to the relationship, to being uncomfortable, to being mad, to whatever happens—but don't give up. Realize the greatest fight is with yourself and it often has little to do with the other person. If it's hysterical it's historical. Breathe. This too will pass if you let it. How important is it? Remember your goal.

The fighting in and of itself can create deeper intimacy if you're willing to walk through it. I sense you want to go further than you ever have. Keep going. Anger is often the sign that you're hitting your own wall. This is good news.

NEGOTIATIONS

I suggest you stay on your side of the street. Focus on what you will do, what you're willing to do, and negotiate from there. Anything you promise to do that you are not already willing to do will become challenging when the heat wears off. Remember, you'll promise almost anything in the beginning and resent it later. If this happens it's not the end of the world. You'll need to renegotiate and stay true to yourself.

If you can't walk, you can't stay. If you can't stay and negotiate, you'll have to start over with someone else.

Solution one. Find a new problem.

Solution two. Stay and fix the problem.

Don't get me wrong, you'll be doing plenty of things you don't want to do, i.e., getting married. Get used to it. Just don't go against yourself.

Avoid resentments. Negotiate first.

Preparations. Where to live. I suggest you live where you live and plan from there. If your place is uninhabitable fix it or move yourself. Preparation is 99 percent you. This is the good news because it's something you can do something about.

Job. Do something that strengthens you as a job. Do it consistently to build discipline and earn consistent money. This is your backbone and you'll need one to go forward.

Career. If you can envision a career, even better, as this creates passion in your life for your life. Not for you wife, for your life. Know where you're going, then ask who is coming with you in that order.

Money. Marriage is a good investment but you'll need start-up capital. Plan ahead to avoid strain on the relationship.

Time. Wait at least a year before you marry. See each other in every season, then decide.

HOT VERSUS BEAUTIFUL

Men often marry for hot and get the bill later. Hot is good for three to six months. If you become addicted it can last indefinitely, as long as you can pay the bill and stand the adrenaline drain.

PLAN ON IT GETTING WORSE

All the things that annoy you, that you fight about, that you're scared of, plan on them getting worse. Except this. Commit to the relationship no matter what and they'll lose their power and importance.

Mature people accept lack of perfection in others.

QUESTION

Is this the last woman I'll have sex with? I say no,
this is the first woman you'll have sex with.
Because you're loved, you'll explore your
masculine and devour her. A whole other world of
archetypal sexuality will open up to you beyond
anything you currently can experience.

ePHOTOS

When my wife suggested we do an ePhoto shoot before the wedding she was met with, and I understate, resistance. I have never liked photos and didn't find myself to be very photogenic. That said, the photo shoot was amazing. Good photographers know how to make you look good. The experience is fun and helps you bond together. It's like being a model for a day. At first it was awkward. By the end of the day you'll want to do it again.

The photos capture you at one of the happiest times of your life. People look good when they're in love and you can see it. The ePhotos create proud memories to share with your friends, which is also fun. It prepares you for your family pictures and for photos on your wedding day. Women love this event. I highly recommend it.

WEDDING PHOTOS

Hire the best photographer, not your friend. I know they're expensive and you'll think it's a waste of money. It's not. We paid $3,000 including the ePhoto session. A seemingly absurd amount of money to me at the time. It was worth it. There really is no other way to capture the event. When the photos are good they add an even more magical quality to the event. Memories, good memories are cornerstones of a relationship. The things you go through together, the way you negotiate, are important.

Take lots of photos with family and friends. Give them copies of themselves. Your family will appreciate it.

THE WEDDING

The wedding is a powerful cornerstone, a turning point in people's lives. It denotes union and partnership. Perhaps for the first time we become willing to venture together. The day that symbolically brings us together is the wedding day.

While it's true that all that matters is the two, it's the many that creates the experience. The family, the friends carry the day. It's their blessings, their witness that deepens and strengthens the bond.

Our lives are a masterpiece of the people in them. They're the gems that mold us.

I encourage people to plan their day, invite their family and friends and experience the exquisite love of others.

I had two weddings. The first in America I thought wouldn't matter, that we could do a civil ceremony, which we did, and be done with it and "go on with our lives".

Luckily I had a wedding day. My wife's beauty, the ceremony, the family and friends who witnessed were priceless. The photos capture a joy and innocence I've never experienced. It's a moment where love is all there is. It expresses our essence.

I wrote a song for my wife. The way people listened, so open, so free of themselves touched me as to how close we are.

Two of my friends performed with love. I watched with so much pleasure and pride as our friends spoke.

Our second wedding was in Taiwan. Since we had done it before and it was all my wife's friends and family I didn't expect much. However, again I experienced this timeless joy with 144 people I didn't know, whose language I barely spoke. Their love, their full attention to us was beautiful beyond words.

At the end of the night when everyone had left, my wife and I experienced an exquisite loneliness. I missed these people I barely knew profoundly. They were pure mirrors of love. With no other intention, just for a moment, reminding us that love is all there is.

I encourage you to have your wedding day to collect your treasures which are the people in your life and keep them close to you, keep their photos, their memories with you.

I encourage you to smile when you hear the words: Congratulations, Congratulations. For you have done something we inherently recognize as precious. Congratulations!

WEDDING SONG

I'm going to love you, that's for sure. And for this there is no cure. I've taken my vow, I've taken my vow. I'm loving you, always loving you.

Burning sun and Milky Way, every night and every day. I've taken my vow, I've taken my vow. I'm loving you, always loving you.

You are the anchor of my soul, teacher of the things I didn't know. If they ask me if my heart is true, I will tell them I'm loving you. I'm always loving you.

ABOUT THE AUTHOR

James Allen Hanrahan

James Allen Hanrahan is a certified ASR Educator and T.A Practitioner. He has studied with renowned relationship expert Dr Pat Allen and Spiritual Psychology pioneers Ron and Mary Hulnick. He also has an extensive background in Hatha Yoga.

For workshops, events, new publications and FREE videos, please go to www.jamesallenhanrahan.com

Printed in Poland
by Amazon Fulfillment
Poland Sp. z o.o., Wrocław

36758129R00078